ARCHER PAUL

DESIGN ALGORITHMS TO SOLVE COMMON PROBLEMS

Mastering Algorithm Design for Practical Solutions (2024 Guide)

Copyright © 2024 by Archer Paul

All rights reserved. No part of this publication may be reproduced, stored or transmitted in any form or by any means, electronic, mechanical, photocopying, recording, scanning, or otherwise without written permission from the publisher. It is illegal to copy this book, post it to a website, or distribute it by any other means without permission.

Archer Paul asserts the moral right to be identified as the author of this work.

First edition

This book was professionally typeset on Reedsy.
Find out more at reedsy.com

Contents

1. Introduction — 1
2. Designing an Algorithm — 3
3. Divide and Conquer — 11
4. Greedy Algorithms — 27
5. Dynamic Programming — 50
6. Branch and Bound — 72
7. Randomized Algorithm — 83
8. Recursion and Backtracking — 90
9. Conclusion — 105

1

Introduction

Algorithms encompass ordered sets of instructions devised to assist in solving specific problems involving calculations, data processing, and automated reasoning. Widely applied in computer science, data science, and information technology, algorithms represent an extremely efficient means expressible within finite space and time.

Their versatility makes them optimal for representing solutions to various problems, regardless of programming language – we've utilized C++ in our examples, but algorithms are language-agnostic. Algorithm design is crucial, emphasizing the creation of an efficient algorithm that minimizes both space and time usage. Different problem-solving approaches exist, some prioritizing time efficiency and others memory efficiency. Balancing both simultaneously is challenging.

Familiar algorithms include those for graphs, sorting, and searching. Search and sort algorithms are foundational, exemplified by the Google Search Engine Algorithm, renowned for ranking web pages by relevance. In the dynamic landscape of data retrieval, algorithms like the hashtag algorithm on social media stand out, demonstrating remarkable speed in searching through vast datasets.

For those seeking to deepen their understanding or embark on a career as a software engineer, delving into algorithm design within data structures is an excellent starting point. This guide targets individuals with a foundational grasp of mathematics and programming, assuming familiarity with basic data structures and algorithms, as it delves into design theory and more intricate algorithms.

2

Designing an Algorithm

Have you ever pondered why Google stands out as the go-to search engine for most people, despite numerous alternatives available? Is it due to speed, aesthetics, or superior search capabilities? The answer may trace back to a pivotal moment when search engines vied for supremacy, with Google's ascent propelled by a distinctive algorithm.

Developed by Google's founders, Larry Page and Sergey Brin, their algorithm, PageRank, revolutionized internet information retrieval. PageRank essentially acted as a popularity gauge, ranking web pages based on inbound links, implying higher importance for pages with more quality links.

In essence, if you searched for information on Borzoi dogs and got a thousand results, PageRank would identify the pages with the most incoming links, assuming their significance. While the concept behind PageRank is straightforward, its implementation involves complex mathematical concepts like eigenvector centrality and row stochastic matrices.

DESIGN ALGORITHMS TO SOLVE COMMON PROBLEMS

Algorithms, defined as systematic sequences of steps to solve problems, serve as the backbone of modern software and hardware. PageRank's success catapulted Google to search engine dominance, anchoring its present-day triumphs.

But what precisely is an algorithm? It's more than a mere sequence of steps; it orchestrates computational processes sans human intervention. Consider baking a cake: rather than relying on subjective judgments like appearance, algorithms depend on objective criteria, such as internal temperature.

Key attributes of algorithms include their granularity, sequence, and automatability. As you delve deeper into computer science, mastering algorithm design empowers you to create increasingly intricate programs, limited only by your dedication to learning and exploration.

Creating an Algorithm

To comprehend the elements of an algorithm, a practical approach involves solving a problem and designing its solution. Let's explore the process by tackling a specific problem: expressing a given number of seconds in hours, minutes, and seconds. Consider a scenario where a friend mentions taking 9331 seconds to travel between locations; we need a program that outputs this duration in hours, minutes, and seconds.

The following steps guide the program development:

1. **Top-Down Design:** Employ top-down design to delineate steps for input, processing, and output. The input,

in this case, is 9331 seconds, necessitating conversion to hours, minutes, and remaining seconds.
2. **Ordered Step Numbering:** Number the steps in the order of execution. This not only aids in understanding the workflow but also ensures the smooth functioning of the entire process.
3. **Pseudocode Creation:** Craft pseudocode, blending the English language with the chosen programming language. The pseudocode should be both readable to individuals unfamiliar with programming and translatable into any programming language. Refining the specific problem's pseudocode involves detailed instructions for obtaining, calculating, and outputting the hours, minutes, and seconds.
4. **Flowchart Design:** Once the algorithm takes shape, a flowchart is indispensable. Utilize code snippets within the flowchart to visualize the process.
5. **Program Implementation:** Writing the actual program becomes straightforward after the algorithm is established. A sample snippet in a programming language (e.g., C++) demonstrates the conversion of seconds to hours, minutes, and seconds.

int secsTotal, secsRemain, hours, minutes, seconds;
　System.out.print("Please enter the total number of seconds: "); // prompt user for total seconds
　hours = secsTotal / 3600; // determine number of hours
　secsRemain = secsTotal % 3600; // determine remaining seconds
　minutes = secsRemain / 60; // determine number of minutes
　seconds = secsRemain % 60; // determine number of seconds

System.out.println("");
System.out.println(secsTotal + " seconds is equivalent to ");
// output hours, minutes, and seconds
System.out.println(hours + " hour(s) - " + minutes + " minute(s) - " + seconds + " second(s).");

This process provides a structured approach to problem-solving and algorithm design. Additionally, it introduces other computer science problems such as factorials, prime numbers, and the Fibonacci sequence, each requiring specific algorithms for effective resolution. The guide encourages understanding and proficiency in algorithm design, reinforcing the foundational aspects of computer science.

Understanding the fundamentals of algorithm design is essential. Let's explore how to tackle a problem and devise its solution.

Problem: Convert a given number of seconds into hours, minutes, and seconds.

Example: Suppose a friend mentions driving for 9331 seconds. We need a program to display this duration in hours, minutes, and seconds.

Here's a step-by-step guide to develop the program:

1. **Top-Down Design:** Begin with a comprehensive overview, covering input, processing, and output stages.
2. **Sequential Numbering:** Arrange steps in the order they execute. This ensures smooth operation.
3. **Pseudocode Creation:** Craft pseudocode blending English with programming language. It should be readable by non-programmers and adaptable to any language.

DESIGNING AN ALGORITHM

Initial pseudocode:

- Obtain total seconds.
- Calculate hours, minutes, and seconds.
- Output results.

Refined version:

- Obtain total seconds.
- Calculate hours (total seconds / 3600).
- Calculate remaining seconds (total seconds % 3600).
- Calculate minutes (remaining seconds / 60).
- Calculate seconds (remaining seconds % 60).
- Output hours, minutes, and seconds.

1. **Flowchart Design:** Translate the algorithm into a visual representation using code snippets.
2. **Program Writing:** Implement the algorithm in code:

```
int secsTotal, secsRemain, hours, minutes, seconds;
    System.out.print("Please enter the total number of seconds: "); //prompt user for total seconds
    hours = secsTotal / 3600; // determine number of hours
    secsRemain = secsTotal % 3600; // determine remaining seconds
    minutes = secsRemain / 60; // determine number of minutes
    seconds = secsRemain % 60; // determine number of seconds
    System.out.println("");
    System.out.println(secsTotal + " seconds is equivalent to "); // output hours, minutes, and seconds
    System.out.println(hours + " hour(s) - " + minutes + " minute(s)
```

- " + seconds + " second(s).");

In addition to this problem, understanding algorithms for factorials, prime numbers, and the Fibonacci sequence is crucial. Factorials, denoted by "n!", represent the product of all integers from 1 to a given number "n."

For example:

- 6! = 6 × 5 × 4 × 3 × 2 × 1 = 720
- 5! = 5 × 4 × 3 × 2 × 1 = 120
- 8! = 8 × 7 × 6 × 5 × 4 × 3 × 2 × 1 = 40,320

Consider designing a program efficiently computing factorials using flowcharts and for loops. By breaking down the process, you can develop a generalized approach applicable to any number.

Algorithm design is foundational in computer science. As you master it, the possibilities for creating innovative programs become limitless.

Prime Numbers

In your high school math lessons, you learned that prime numbers are those divisible only by themselves and 1, meaning there are no remainders when divided by another number. For instance, 12 is divisible by 6 (12 % 6 = 0), but 23 is not divisible by 6 (23 % 6 = 5). Prime numbers play a crucial role in computer science, contributing to data encryption and random number generation.

Consider verifying if 13 is prime. Although you know it is, the process involves checking divisibility by numbers up to half of 13. A more efficient program could skip unnecessary calculations, focusing on dividing by numbers up to half its value.

Fibonacci Sequence

The Fibonacci sequence initiates with 0 and 1, each subsequent number being the sum of the preceding two. Represented as a rule, it is $X_{n-1} + X_{n-2}$. Visualizing the sequence as a spiral highlights its progressive pattern, demonstrating that each number, excluding the first two, results from adding the previous two.

An algorithm employing a for loop and variables (X_n, X_{n-1}, and X_{n-2}) can generate this sequence.

Algorithm Design Techniques

Several algorithm design techniques are noteworthy:

1. **Divide and Conquer:** A top-down approach where the original problem is divided, solved individually, and then combined for an overall solution.

2. **Greedy Technique:** Addresses optimization problems by choosing solutions based on immediate benefits, without guaranteeing the optimal solution.

3. **Dynamic Programming:** A bottom-up strategy solving smaller problems before aggregating them into a solution for a larger problem, beneficial for a considerable number of subproblems.

4. **Branch and Bound:** Utilized for non-convex problems, divides subproblems into at least two restricted subproblems. Can be slow in the worst case due to growing effort with problem size.

5. **Randomized Algorithms**: Incorporates unbiased, independent random bits to influence the algorithm's computation.

6. **Backtracking Algorithm:** Exhaustively explores possibilities until finding the correct solution, backtracking when alternatives prove unsuccessful.

With these approaches, the focus shifts to the first design technique – divide and conquer.

3

Divide and Conquer

In this chapter, we will explore the Divide and Conquer technique and delve into some algorithms falling under its purview, elucidating how this approach aids in problem-solving. The technique can be dissected into three integral components:

1. **Divide**:The problem is fragmented into smaller, more manageable subproblems.
2. **Conquer**:The smaller subproblems are systematically addressed through recursive procedures.
3. **Combine**: The solutions to the smaller subproblems are integrated to derive the solution for the overarching problem.

Several standard algorithms fall within the scope of Divide and Conquer, with Quicksort being one such example. Quicksort, a Divide and Conquer (DAC) algorithm, selects a specific element as its pivot and orchestrates the partitioning of an array around this chosen pivot. There exist various versions of Quicksort, each employing distinct methods for pivot selection:

- Choosing the first element as the pivot.
    - Choosing the last element as the pivot.
    - Opting for a random element as the pivot.
    - Selecting the median as the pivot.

The recursive Quicksort function employs pseudocode to articulate its logic, with a key role played by the Partition Algorithm. This algorithm strategically places the chosen pivot at the correct position in the sorted array, arranging smaller elements to its left and larger elements to its right. The pseudocode for the partitioning process involves iterating through array elements, determining the smaller elements' indices, and effecting swaps as needed.

To illustrate the partitioning process, consider an array and step through the iterations, showcasing the element swaps and the eventual correct positioning of the pivot.

The chapter also provides the implementation of Quicksort in C++, featuring functions for swapping elements, partitioning, and the main Quicksort procedure. A driver code demonstrates the application of Quicksort to an array, producing a sorted output.

This comprehensive exploration of the Divide and Conquer technique and its Quicksort application equips readers with a robust understanding of this pivotal algorithmic approach.

Recursive Quicksort Pseudocode and Partition Algorithm

Recursive Quicksort Pseudocode:

```
/* low —> Starting index, high —> Ending index */
Quicksort(arr[], low, high)
{
if (low < high)
{
/* pi is partitioning index, arr[pi] is now
at right place */
pi = partition(arr, low, high);
Quicksort(arr, low, pi - 1); // Before pi
Quicksort(arr, pi + 1, high); // After pi
}
}
```

Partition Algorithm Pseudocode:

```
/* low —> Starting index, high —> Ending index */
partition (arr[], low, high)
{
// pivot (the element placed at the correct position in the array)
  pivot = arr[high];
  i = (low - 1) // The smaller element's index, indicating the pivot's correct position so far
  for (j = low; j <= high- 1; j++)
  {
  // If the current element is smaller than the pivot
  if (arr[j] < pivot)
  {
  i++; // the smaller element's index is incremented
  swap arr[i] and arr[j]
  }
```

}
swap arr[i + 1] and arr[high])
return (i + 1)
}

Illustration of Partition() with Example: Consider an array **arr[]** = {10, 80, 30, 90, 40, 50, 70}.

- Indexes: 0 1 2 3 4 5 6
- **low = 0, high = 6, pivot = arr[h] = 70**
- Initialize the smaller element's index, **i = -1**
- Traverse elements from **j = low** to **high-1**
- **j = 0**: Since **arr[j] <= pivot**, increment **i** and swap(**arr[i], arr[j]**)
- **i = 0, arr[]** = {10, 80, 30, 90, 40, 50, 70}
- **j = 1**: Since **arr[j] > pivot**, no change in **i** and **arr[]**
- **j = 2**: Since **arr[j] <= pivot**, increment **i** and swap(**arr[i], arr[j]**)
- **i = 1, arr[]** = {10, 30, 80, 90, 40, 50, 70}
- Continue similarly for **j = 3** to **j = 5**
- Because **j** is equal to **high-1**, exit the loop
- Swap **arr[i+1]** with **arr[high]** to put the pivot in its correct position
- **arr[]** = {10, 30, 40, 50, 70, 90, 80}

Implementation in C++:
    // C++ implementation of QuickSort
    // ... (Refer to the provided code for the full implementation)
    Output:
    Sorted array:
    1 5 7 8 9 10
    This code snippet showcases the pseudocode and practical

implementation of the Quicksort algorithm, a powerful sorting technique with applications in various computing scenarios.

Quicksort Examination

Analyzing the efficiency of Quicksort involves expressing its time complexity through the following equation:
$$T(n) = T(k) + T(n-k-1) + (n)$$

In this formula, the first two terms signify recursive calls, while the last term represents the partition process. The variable k denotes the number of elements smaller than the pivot. The time complexity relies on the chosen partition strategy and the input array. Here are details for three scenarios:

Worst Case:

The worst case arises when the partition selects the smallest or largest element as the pivot. For instance, when the pivot is always the last element, and the array is already sorted, the recurrence is:
$$T(n) = T(0) + T(n-1) + (n)$$
Simplified, this becomes:
$$T(n) = T(n-1) + (n)$$
Resulting in:
$$O(n^2)$$

Best Case:

The best case occurs when the middle element is consistently chosen as the pivot. The recurrence is:
$$T(n) = 2T(n/2) + (n)$$
Leading to a solution of:
$$O(n \log n)$$

Average Case:

Conducting an average case analysis involves considering all possible array permutations. A rough estimation considers placing $O(n/9)$ elements in one set and $O(9n/10)$ elements in another during the partition process. The recurrence is:
$$T(n) = T(n/9) + T(9n/10) + (n)$$
Resulting in a solution of:
$$O(n \log n)$$

Quicksort's worst-case time complexity is $O(n^2)$, but its practical efficiency surpasses other algorithms like Heapsort and Mergesort. The inner loop's efficiency and the flexibility to change pivot choices contribute to its speed. In dealing with massive externally stored data, Mergesort may be preferred.

Quicksort is an in-place sorting algorithm, utilizing minimal extra space for recursive calls. An interesting variation is the 3-way Quicksort, which efficiently handles arrays with redundant elements by dividing them into three segments.

Comparatively, Quicksort and Mergesort have distinct characteristics. Quicksort excels in practicality, especially when using the randomized version with $O(n \log n)$ time complexity. Randomized Quicksort's cache-friendly nature enhances its performance with arrays. However, Mergesort, despite its $O(n \log n)$ average complexity, demands additional storage, making it less suitable for arrays. The distinction becomes more pronounced with linked lists, where memory allocation differs significantly.

In arrays, random access is possible, providing an advantage for Quicksort due to its continuous memory structure. Linked lists, on the other hand, benefit Mergesort operations, as they allow insertions in $O(1)$ time without requiring extra space. Quicksort exhibits higher overhead in scenarios where random access is not feasible, emphasizing the impact of data structure on sorting algorithm choice.

Mergesort Overview

The Mergesort algorithm, falling under the Divide and Conquer (DAC) technique, stands out as a powerful tool for constructing recursive algorithms. This approach involves breaking down a problem into two distinct segments, solving them independently, and then merging the solutions to obtain the overall answer.

Consider an array A that needs sorting within a specific range, starting at index p and ending at index r, denoted as A[p...r]. The process involves three key steps:

1. **Divide:** Assume q as the midpoint between p and r, splitting the subarray A[p..r] into two: A[p...q] and A[q+1,

DESIGN ALGORITHMS TO SOLVE COMMON PROBLEMS

r].
2. **Conquer:** Once the array is split, both subarrays undergo individual sorting. If the base condition is not met, the procedure repeats, recursively splitting and sorting the subarrays.
3. **Combine:** Upon reaching the base condition, the sorted subarrays merge into one comprehensive sorted subarray.

The Mergesort algorithm persists in dividing an array into subarrays until a specified condition is met. Mergesort can operate on a subarray of size 1, i.e., when p equals r. The sorted subarrays are progressively combined into larger arrays until the entire array is sorted.

Here's a representation of the algorithm:
If $p < r$
Then $q \rightarrow (p + r) / 2$
MERGE-SORT(A, p, q)
MERGE-SORT(A, q+1, r)
MERGE(A, p, q, r)

The **MergeSort(A, 0, length(A)-1)** function is invoked to sort the array. The algorithm recursively divides the array until it meets the base condition of having only a single element. The **merge** function then merges these sorted subarrays to achieve the complete array sorting.

Merge Function:
FUNCTION MERGE(A, p, q, r)
n1 = q - p + 1
n2 = r - q
Create arrays L[1...n1+1] and R[1...n2+1]
For i ← 1 to n1
L[i] ← A[p + i - 1]

DIVIDE AND CONQUER

For j ← 1 to n2
R[j] ← A[q + j]
L[n1 + 1] ← ∞
R[n2 + 1] ← ∞
i ← 1
j ← 1
For k ← p to r
If L[i] ≤ R[j]
Then A[k] ← L[i]
i ← i + 1
Else A[k] ← R[j]
j ← j + 1

The Merge step in recursive algorithms relies on a base case and its merging capability for results from those cases. Mergesort follows this principle, emphasizing the significance of the merge step.

During the merge step:

- Three pointers are maintained for each subarray.
- The final array has a pointer for its current index.
- The process involves comparing current elements of both arrays, copying the smaller element to the sorted arrays, and adjusting pointers accordingly.
- This continues until one array is fully traversed, at which point the remaining elements from the non-empty array are copied.

The step-by-step process of the **merge()** function involves dividing the array iteratively until atomic values are reached, maintaining the order of elements. Subsequently, the subarrays are merged in a way consistent with their division, leading to a fully sorted array.

In summary, Mergesort's strength lies in its systematic division, conquering of subproblems, and efficient merging, providing a reliable method for sorting arrays.

Mergesort Analysis

Consider the time complexity T(n) of the Mergesort algorithm. Sorting the two divided halves takes a maximum of 2T time. When merging the sorted lists, there are a total of n-1 comparisons, as the last remaining element needs to be copied into the combined list, requiring no comparison. Thus, the relational formula can be expressed as +(n-1), with the -1 being disregarded due to the time taken to copy the element into the merge lists.

In the best-case scenario, where the array is already sorted, the time complexity is O(n*log n). The average-case time complexity is O(n*log n), occurring when at least two elements are not in ascending or descending order. The worst-case time complexity is O(n*log n), happening when an array sorted in descending order is transformed into ascending order. The space complexity of the mergesort algorithm is O(n).

Closest Pair of Points

Consider an array of n points in the plane, with the task of finding the closest pair of points, a common problem in applications like air traffic control for detecting potential collisions. The distance between two points, p and q, is calculated using the formula.

The brute force solution, with a time complexity of $O(n^2)$, involves computing the distance between each pair and returning the smallest. Utilizing the Divide and Conquer strategy, the time complexity is optimized to $O(n*\log n)$.

For an alternative approach with a time complexity of $O(n*(\log n)^2)$, the algorithm follows these steps:

1. Pre-process by sorting the input array based on x coordinates.
2. Find the middle point of the array, considering it as P[n/2].
3. Divide the array into two halves: the first from P[0] to P[n/2] and the second from P[n/2+1] to P[n-1].
4. Recursively find the smallest distance in each subarray, obtaining dl and dr, and determine the minimum d among them.
5. Consider the vertical line passing through P[n/2], identifying points with x coordinates closer to that line than d, and create an array strip[] of these points.
6. Sort the array strip[] based on y coordinates, optimizing the process to O(n) by recursive sorting and merging.

7. Find the smallest distance in strip[], which is O(n) rather than the apparent O(m^2), where m is the size of strip[], by geometrically proving that each point only needs checking against a maximum of 7 points after it when the array is sorted by y coordinates.
8. Return the minimum of d along with the distance calculated in step 7.

Implementation

Here's the C++ implementation of the algorithm:

```
#include
using namespace std;

// A structure representing a Point in the 2D plane
class Point {
public:
int x, y;
};

// Functions required for the library function qsort()
int compareX(const void* a, const void* b) {
Point* p1 = (Point*)a, * p2 = (Point*)b;
return (p1->x - p2->x);
}

int compareY(const void* a, const void* b) {
Point* p1 = (Point*)a, * p2 = (Point*)b;
return (p1->y - p2->y);
}

float dist(Point p1, Point p2) {
```

```
    return sqrt((p1.x - p2.x) * (p1.x - p2.x) +
    (p1.y - p2.y) * (p1.y - p2.y));
}

float bruteForce(Point P[], int n) {
    float min = FLT_MAX;
    for (int i = 0; i < n; ++i)
    for (int j = i + 1; j < n; ++j)
    if (dist(P[i], P[j]) < min)
    min = dist(P[i], P[j]);
    return min;
}

float min(float x, float y) {
    return (x < y) ? x : y;
}

float stripClosest(Point strip[], int size, float d) {
    float min = d;
    qsort(strip, size, sizeof(Point), compareY);
    for (int i = 0; i < size; ++i)
    for (int j = i + 1; j < size && (strip[j].y - strip[i].y) < min; ++j)
    if (dist(strip[i], strip[j]) < min)
    min = dist(strip[i], strip[j]);
    return min;
}

float closestUtil(Point P[], int n) {
    if (n <= 3)
    return bruteForce(P, n);
    int mid = n / 2;
```

```
Point midPoint = P[mid];
float dl = closestUtil(P, mid);
float dr = closestUtil(P + mid, n - mid);
float d = min(dl, dr);
Point strip[n];
int j = 0;
for (int i = 0; i < n; i++)
if (abs(P[i].x - midPoint.x) < d)
strip[j] = P[i], j++;
return min(d, stripClosest(strip, j, d));
}

float closest(Point P[], int n) {
    qsort(P, n, sizeof(Point), compareX);
    return closestUtil(P, n);
}

int main() {
    Point P[] = {{2, 3}, {12, 30}, {40, 50}, {5, 1}, {12, 10}, {3, 4}};
    int n = sizeof(P) / sizeof(P[0]);
    cout « "The smallest distance is " « closest(P, n);
    return 0;
}
```
Output:
The smallest distance is 1.414214

Time Complexity

Consider the time complexity of the algorithm denoted as T(n), assuming the sorting algorithm follows O(n Log n). The algorithm divides points into two sets and recursively calls for both. After division, the strip is found in O(n) time and sorted in O(n Log n) time, with closest points determined in O(n) time.

DIVIDE AND CONQUER

The time complexity expression, T(n), can be represented as:
$()=2(2)+()+(\log\ )+()T(n)=2T(2n)+O(n)+O(n\log n)+O(n)\ ()=2(2)+(\log\ )\ ()=(\log\ \log\ )T(n)=T(n\log n\log n)$

Notes

1. Optimizing the fifth step in the algorithm can improve time complexity to O(n Log n).
2. The code can find the smallest distance and can be adapted to find all points with the smallest distance.
3. Quicksort is utilized, with a worst-case of $O(n^2)$. Alternatively, O(Log n) sorting algorithms like Heapsort or Mergesort can provide an upper bound of $O(n (\log n)^2)$.

What Doesn't Qualify as Divide and Conquer?

Binary Search is not a divide and conquer algorithm; it's a sorting algorithm. In each step, it compares input element x with the array's middle element. If values match, the middle index is returned. If x is smaller, it recurs for the left side; otherwise, for the right side. Binary Search, falling under Decrease and Conquer, doesn't qualify as divide and conquer since each step has only one subproblem, while divide and conquer requires at least two.

Divide and Conquer Algorithm:

(„)DAC(a,i,j)

if small(a, i, j)return Solution(a, i, j)else=divide(a, i, j)=DAC(a, i, mid)=DAC(a, mid+1, j)=combine(b, c)return dif small(a, i, j)return Solution(a, i, j)elsem=divide(a, i, j)b=DAC(a, i, mid)c=DAC(a, mid+1, j)d=combine(b, c)return d

Recurrence relation: $()=1()+2(2)+2()T(n)=f1(n)+2T(2n)+f2(n)$

Example: To find the minimum and maximum element of a specified array: Input: {70, 250, 50, 80, 140, 12, 14} Output:

Minimum: 12, Maximum: 250

Approach: For Maximum, a recursive approach is used with a condition to find the maximum element on both sides. For Minimum, a similar recursive approach is employed with conditions to find the minimum element. The implementation includes C++ code demonstrating the Divide and Conquer Algorithm.

Output:
Maximum: 250
Minimum: 12

Advantages of Divide and Conquer:

1. Solves complex problems effectively, exemplified by the Tower of Hanoi puzzle.
2. Efficient utilization of cache memory, reducing space requirements.
3. More proficient than brute force techniques.
4. Prohibits parallelism, eliminating the need for modifications for parallel processing.

Disadvantages of Divide and Conquer:

1. High memory management due to recursive design.
2. Explicit stacks may overuse space.
3. Rigorous recursion beyond the CPU stack capacity may lead to system crashes.

In the next chapter, we delve into greedy algorithms.

4

Greedy Algorithms

Algorithm design does not offer a universal solution for every problem; the choice of technique depends on the specific nature of the problem. While there might be multiple options in certain cases, there will always be an optimal technique. A proficient programmer discerns the most suitable technique for a given situation, and among these, greedy algorithms are just one option.

A Greedy algorithm, primarily a technique rather than a specific algorithm, operates based on making choices that seem optimal at the time. It prioritizes logically optimal decisions at each step, aiming for a globally optimal solution. The technique ensures optimization of an objective function, which requires either maximization or minimization at a particular point. Notably, a greedy algorithm makes irreversible choices during its computation, without the ability to revise decisions.

Like all methodologies, greedy algorithms come with their set of advantages and disadvantages. On the positive side:

1. Greedy algorithms are relatively easy to find for a given problem, and multiple approaches may prove effective.
2. Analyzing runtime for greedy algorithms is typically more straightforward compared to other techniques. For instance, in the Divide and Conquer approach, runtime analysis can be challenging due to the changing nature of subproblems at each recursion level.
3. However, the challenge with greedy algorithms lies in understanding correctness issues. Even when the correct algorithm is identified, proving its correctness is more of an art than a science, demanding creativity.

It's noteworthy that only a limited number of greedy algorithms are genuinely correct, but further exploration of this aspect will be covered later.

Designing a Greedy Algorithm:

Imagine a scenario where you have limited time, denoted by T, and a list of tasks represented by an array A, where each element signifies the completion time for a specific task. The goal is to maximize the number of tasks you can accomplish within the given time frame.

This problem lends itself to a simple greedy algorithm. During each iteration, the algorithm makes a choice favoring the task with the minimum time to finish. Throughout this process, two variables, numberOfThings and currentTime, are maintained. The steps involve sorting array A in non-decreasing order, selecting each task one at a time, adding its completion time to currentTime, and incrementing num-

GREEDY ALGORITHMS

berOfThings. This process continues as long as currentTime is equal to or less than T.

Consider the array A = {5, 3, 4, 2, 1} and T = 6. After sorting A, the iterations show the progression of currentTime and numberOfThings. The final answer is 3.

Implementation:

Here's an implementation in C++ to solve the described problem. The program reads inputs, sorts the array, and iterates through the tasks, updating currentTime and numberOfThings accordingly.

```
#include
#include
using namespace std;

const int MAX = 105;
    int A[MAX];

int main()
    {
    int T, N, numberOfThings = 0, currentTime = 0;
    cin >> N >> T;

for(int i = 0; i < N; ++i)
    cin >> A[i];

sort(A, A + N);

for(int i = 0; i < N; ++i)
    {
    currentTime += A[i];
    if(currentTime > T)
```

```
    break;
    numberOfThings++;
}
```

```
cout « numberOfThings « endl;
    return 0;
}
```

This is a straightforward example, demonstrating how a greedy algorithm can be applied once the problem is understood.

Complex Scheduling Problem:

Now, let's consider a more intricate scheduling problem. Given a list of tasks, their completion times, and priorities (weights), the objective is to determine the optimal order for task completion. The input includes the number of jobs (N), priority list (P), and time list (T) for each job.

To optimize, the total time required for task completion is calculated as $C(j) = T[1] + T[2] + ... + T[j]$, where $1 <= j <= N$. The objective function, F, represents the weighted sum of all completion times: $F = P[1] * C(1) + P[2] * C(2) + ... + P[N] * C(N)$. The goal is to minimize this objective function.

This scheduling problem poses multiple objective functions, and finding the best approach depends on the specific criteria for optimization. The ultimate aim is to minimize the weighted sum of completion times for an efficient solution.

Examining Special Cases:

Let's delve into a couple of distinctive scenarios that exhibit an intuitive approach to optimal solutions. These special cases pave the way for identifying natural greedy algorithms, prompting the subsequent task of selecting the appropriate one and substantiating its correctness.

These two special cases are outlined as follows:

1. **Equal Completion Times (Case 1):** When the time required to complete all tasks is identical ($T[i] = T[j]$ for $1 <= i, j <= N$), but the priorities differ, determining a sensible task scheduling order becomes essential.
2. **Equal Priorities (Case 2):** If all tasks share the same priorities ($P[i] = P[j]$ for $1 <= N$), but their completion times vary, the challenge lies in deciding the order of task execution.

In the first case, when completion times are the same, preference should be given to the task with the highest priority. For the second case, when tasks have different priorities, prioritizing the task with the shortest completion time is optimal.

Case 1:

To minimize the objective function, assuming completion time for each task is t ($T[i] = t$ for $1 <= i <= N$), associating the highest priority with the shortest completion time is essential. The completion times follow the pattern $C(1) = t$, $C(2) = 2 * t$, $C(3) = 3 * t$, and so forth.

Case 2:

When tasks possess different priorities but share the same

completion time, the objective function F = P[1] * C(1) + P[2] * C(2) + ... + P[N] * C(N) can be minimized by commencing with tasks requiring the shortest completion time.

Generalization:

Moving beyond special cases, where completion time and priority differ for each task, determining the optimal solution involves addressing conflicting advice from the rules. A simple mathematical function can aggregate time and priority into a single score. Two simple algorithms are presented - Algorithm 1 orders tasks by decreasing value of (P[i] - T[i]), while Algorithm 2 orders tasks by decreasing value of (P[i] / T[i]).

Choosing between these algorithms is crucial, and to illustrate, an example with tasks T = {5, 2} and priorities P = {3, 1} is analyzed. Algorithm 1 suggests completing task 2 first, resulting in F = 23. Algorithm 2, however, recommends task 1 first, yielding F = 22. The correctness of Algorithm 2 is established, while Algorithm 1 is ruled out.

It's important to note that greedy algorithms are often incorrect, and while Algorithm 1 is discarded, it doesn't guarantee Algorithm 2's correctness universally. The proposed algorithm returns the optimal value for the objective function:

Algorithm(P, T, N) {
　let S be an array of pairs (C++ STL pair) storing scores and indices,
　C be completion times, and F be the objective function.
　for i from 1 to N:
　S[i] = (P[i] / T[i], i) // Algorithm 2
　sort(S)
　C = 0

```
F = 0
for i from 1 to N: // Greedily make the best choice
    C = C + T[S[i].second]
    F = F + P[S[i].second] * C
return F
}
```

Time Complexity Analysis:

The computational efficiency of the algorithm can be assessed through time complexity analysis. Here, two loops operate in $O(N)$ time, coupled with a sorting function taking $O(N * \log N)$ time. Consequently, the overall time complexity is $O(2 * N + N * \log N)$ or more succinctly, $O(N * \log N)$.

Establishing Correctness:

To validate the correctness of the second algorithm, a proof by contradiction is employed. Assuming the greedy algorithm fails to produce an optimal solution, a contradictory scenario is derived. Let A represent the output of the greedy schedule (not optimal), and B signify the optimal schedule. Two key assumptions are made: firstly, that all $(P[i] / T[i])$ are distinct, and secondly, $(P[1] / T[1]) > (P[2] / T[2]) > ... > (P[N] / T[N])$.

Assumption 2 ensures the greedy schedule A is (1, 2, 3). As A is not optimal and not equal to B, there must be consecutive jobs in B (i, j) with i > j. This holds true as A = (1, 2, 3, ..., N) is the sole schedule with ascending indices.

Considering the impact of swapping tasks i and j on completion times reveals two cases for another task k:

1. When k is to the left of i and j in B, the swap has no effect on k's completion time.
2. When k is to the right of i and j in B, after the swap, k's completion time becomes C(k) = T[1] + T[2] + ... + T[j] to T[i] − k remains the same.

Analyzing completion times for i and j post-swap shows an increase in i's completion time by T[j] and a decrease in j's completion time by T[i]. This results in a loss (P[i] / T[i]) < (P[j] / T[j]). The assumption (P[i] / T[i]) < (P[j] / T[j]) from Assumption 2 implies (P[i] * T[j]) < (P[j] * T[i]), indicating Loss < Profit. Although B benefits from the swap, it contradicts the assumption of B's optimality, concluding the proof.

Applications of Greedy Algorithms:

For a greedy algorithm to be effective, two components are essential:

1. **Optimal substructures:** Every optimal solution for a problem contains optimal solutions to its subproblems.
2. **Greedy property:** Optimal choices at each step, without reconsidering prior choices, result in a global optimal solution.

Illustrating these properties is the Activity Selection Problem, a combinatorial optimization issue focusing on selecting non-conflicting activities within a specified timeframe. It involves activities with start times (Si) and finish times (fi). A greedy algorithm efficiently solves this problem, ensuring an optimal solution consistently. The algorithm's iterative version is presented below:

Greedy-Iterative-Activity-Selector(A, s, f):
Sort A by finish times stored in f
S = {A[1]}
k = 1
n = A.length
for i = 2 to n:
if s[i] ≥ f[k]:
S = S U {A[i]}
k = i
return S

This algorithm, combining greedy and iterative features, selects non-conflicting activities based on increasing finish times, ensuring an optimal solution each time.

Proof of Optimal Solution:

Consider a set of activities S = {1, 2, ..., n} arranged in order of finish time. Assuming the optimal solution is A ⊆ S with activities ordered by finish time and A's initial activity having an index k ≠ 1 (i.e., the greedy choice is not utilized for the optimal solution). Now, let's demonstrate that B = (A \ {k}) ∪ {1} is also an optimal solution, starting with the greedy choice.

Since $f_1 < f_k$ and the activities in array A are disjoint, B's activities are likewise disjoint. As both A and B contain the same number of activities (|A| = |B|), we can assert that B is optimal.

Once the greedy choice is made, the problem transforms into finding the optimal solution for the subproblem. If the optimal solution for our primary problem S, with the greedy choice resulting in A, then the optimal solution for the selection problem is:

$=(\backslash\{\})\cup\{1\} B=(A\backslash\{k\})\cup\{1\}$

Why? If this were not true, and a solution B' for S' had to be chosen with more activities than A' (the greedy choice for S'), adding 1 to B' would yield a solution B for S with more activities than A. This contradicts feasibility and optimality.

Weighted Activity Selection:

Expanding to a weighted version of the selection problem involves choosing a set of non-overlapping activities to maximize the total weight. Unlike the unweighted problem, there isn't a straightforward greedy solution. However, a dynamic programming approach can be employed.

Assume an optimal solution with activity k; we can recursively find solutions for the non-overlapping sets on the left and right of k due to optimal substructure. This results in an $O(n^3)$ solution. Further optimization is possible by utilizing the optimal solution for each activity set in (i, j) if the solution for (i, t) is known (where t is the final non-overlapping interval with j in (i, j)). This leads to an $O(n^2)$ solution. By considering only ranges (1, j), an $O(n \log n)$ solution is achieved, as illustrated in the algorithm below:

Weighted-Activity-Selection(S): // S = list of activities
sort S by finish time
opt[0] = 0
for i = 1 to n:
t = binary search to find activity with finish time <= start

time for i
   opt[i] = MAX(opt[i-1], opt[t] + w(i))
   return opt[n]

Fractional Knapsack Problem:

The fractional knapsack problem involves filling a container with fractional portions of materials to maximize their value. This differs from the classic knapsack problem, allowing fractional quantities for each material. The problem can be solved in polynomial time, demonstrating how subtle changes impact computational complexity.

In this problem, materials have weight (w_i) and value (v_i), and the goal is to select amounts ($x_i < w_i$) to ensure total benefit maximization. The fractional knapsack problem can be addressed with a greedy algorithm, selecting materials based on their value per unit weight and allowing fractional quantities. The time complexity is $O(n \log n)$, but this can be optimized to $O(n)$ with adaptations, such as finding weighted medians.

Examples of Greedy Algorithms:

The greedy approach proves highly effective in solving various problems, with several algorithms showcasing its applications.

Minimum Spanning Tree:

The Minimum Spanning Tree (MST), also known as the minimum weight spanning tree, constitutes a subset encompassing all edges of an undirected graph. This graph is both connected and edge-weighted, with all vertices linked, devoid of cycles, and boasting the minimum possible total edge weight.

MSTs find utility in diverse scenarios. For instance, a telecommunications company laying cable in a new neighborhood, constrained by specific routes, can model the cable connection points as a graph. Some connections may incur higher costs due to depth or length, reflecting as larger weighted edges in the graph. An MST derived from this graph provides the least expensive route without cycles.

Consider a connected, undirected graph $G = (V, E)$. The spanning tree for G includes all its vertices and constitutes a subgraph with all its edges. The cost of the spanning tree is the sum of edge weights, and the MST is the one with the lowest cost. MSTs find direct application in network design, impacting problems like the Traveling Salesman, Multi-terminal minimum cut, Minimum-cost weighted perfect matching, Cluster analysis, Image segmentation, and Handwriting recognition.

Notable algorithms for finding MSTs include Kruskal's and Prim's algorithms.

Kruskal's Algorithm:

Kruskal's algorithm constructs a spanning tree by iteratively adding edges with the lowest weights, following the greedy approach. The algorithm entails sorting the graph's edges by weight, progressively adding edges to the spanning tree, and ensuring they don't form cycles or have disconnected components.

To check if two vertices are connected, Disjoint Sets offer an efficient solution. These sets have empty intersections, indicating no common elements. Kruskal's algorithm starts with the lowest weighted edges, proceeds to higher weights, and avoids edges that would create cycles. This process continues until the minimum spanning tree is obtained.

Here's an implementation of Kruskal's algorithm in C++:

// (Code implementation provided)

This algorithm selects edges in increasing order of weight, effectively building the minimum spanning tree for a connected, undirected graph.

These examples illustrate the versatility and efficacy of greedy algorithms, particularly in solving graph-related problems.

Time Complexity:

The most time-consuming operation in this algorithm is the sorting process. This is primarily due to the Disjoint operations having an overall complexity of $O(E \log V)$, which aligns with Kruskal's time complexity.

Prim's Algorithm:

Also known as Jarnik's algorithm, Prim's algorithm adheres to a greedy approach for identifying the minimum spanning tree in a weighted, undirected graph. This involves selecting a subset of edges forming a tree with all vertices, minimizing the total weight of the edges in the tree. The algorithm constructs the tree incrementally, starting from an arbitrary vertex and adding the least expensive connection to another vertex at each step.

Algorithm Steps:

1. Maintain two disjoint sets of vertices—one with vertices from the growing spanning tree and the other with vertices not yet included.
2. Select the least expensive vertex from those connected to the spanning tree but not part of it. This is usually done using a Priority Queue, where vertices to be added are inserted.
3. Ensure there are no cycles by marking the already selected nodes and inserting the unmarked nodes into the Priority Queue.

Example Illustration:

In this algorithm, initiation occurs with an arbitrary node, marking it. Subsequent iterations mark new vertices adjacent to already-marked vertices. The greedy nature of Prim's algorithm involves selecting the least expensive edge and marking the associated vertex. For instance, when faced with choices of edges with weights 3, 4, and 5, selecting weight 3 would lead to a cycle, prompting the choice of weight 4. This results in a minimum spanning tree with a total cost of 7, calculated as 1 + 2 + 4.

Implementation:

Here's a code implementation of Prim's algorithm in C++, where a Priority Queue is utilized to efficiently select minimum-weight edges:

// (Code implementation provided)

This implementation effectively showcases the steps of Prim's algorithm, emphasizing its greedy nature and efficiency in constructing a minimum spanning tree.

Time Complexity:

The time complexity of Prim's algorithm is $O((V + E) \log V)$. This arises because each vertex entering the Priority Queue undergoes a single insertion operation, and these insertions have a logarithmic time complexity.

Dijkstra's Algorithm:

Dijkstra's algorithm serves various purposes, with its primary application being the determination of the shortest path between two vertices in a graph while minimizing the total edge weights. The algorithm proceeds through specific steps:

1. Set all vertices' distances to infinity, except for the source vertex, which is set to 0.
2. Push the source vertex into a min-priority queue in the format (distance, vertex), as the comparison is based on vertex distances.
3. Pop the vertex with the minimum distance from the priority queue (initially, the source vertex).
4. Update the distances between the popped vertex and

connected vertices if the current vertex distance + edge weight is less than the next vertex distance. Insert the vertex with the new distance into the priority queue.
5. Skip the process if the popped vertex has been previously visited.
6. Repeat the algorithm until the priority queue is empty.

Implementation (Assuming the source vertex is 1):

// (Code implementation provided)

Time Complexity:

Dijkstra's algorithm has a total time complexity of $O(V^2)$. However, when utilizing the min-priority queue, this reduces to $O(V + E \log V)$. Despite this efficiency, finding the shortest path between all pairs of vertices using this algorithm becomes costly in terms of time. An alternative algorithm designed for such scenarios will be discussed in the dynamic programming chapter.

Graph Coloring Greedy Algorithm:

Graph coloring, a facet of graph theory, involves assigning colors (labels) to graph elements while adhering to specific constraints. Vertex coloring ensures adjacent vertices do not share the same color, while edge coloring assigns unique colors to adjacent edges. Face coloring in planar graphs colors regions or faces so that neighboring faces sharing a boundary have distinct colors.

Key Concepts:

- Chromatic Number: Represents the minimum number of colors needed to color the graph (e.g., 3).
- Vertex Coloring: Indicates the starting point for coloring problems. Edge and face coloring problems can often be transformed into vertex coloring problems.

Origin:

The practice of using colors originated from coloring world maps, where each country was filled with a distinct color. This concept was later generalized to coloring faces in plane-embedded graphs, which extended to coloring vertices through planar duality. In mathematical and computer representation, colors are typically represented by non-negative or positive integers.

Pseudocode:

1. Color the first vertex with the first color.
2. Color the remaining vertices similarly.
3. Color the currently chosen vertex with the lowest-numbered color not used on adjacent colored vertices.
4. If any adjacent vertex to v has used colors, assign a new color to v.

Implementation:

// (Code implementation provided)
   Time Complexity:
In the worst-case scenario, the time complexity for the graph coloring greedy algorithm is $O(V^2 + E)$, where V represents vertices and E represents edges.

Applications:

Greedy coloring algorithms find diverse applications in various domains:

1. **Timetabling or Scheduling:** Creating a schedule for a university's exams involves a graph coloring problem. The subjects form vertices, and shared students create edges. Scheduling exams without overlapping requires determining the graph's chromatic number, representing the minimum time slots.
2. **Mobile Radio Frequencies Assignment:** Assigning frequencies to radio towers demands a graph coloring approach. Towers, represented as vertices, have edges between close towers. The minimum number of frequencies needed to avoid interference corresponds to the graph's chromatic number.
3. **Mobile Radio Frequency Assignment:** Similar to the above, assigning frequencies to towers at the same location necessitates a graph coloring strategy. Each tower is a vertex, and edges between towers within range imply the need for different frequencies. The minimum required frequencies align with the graph's chromatic number.

4. **Sudoku:** Sudoku problems align with graph coloring, where cells are vertices. An edge between two vertices signifies their shared block, row, or column.
5. **Register Allocation:** Compiler organization involves register allocation, assigning numerous target variables to a limited number of CPU registers.
6. **Bipartite Graphs:** Graphs can be tested for bipartiteness through graph coloring. If a graph can be colored with two colors, it is bipartite; otherwise, it is not.
7. **Map Coloring:** Geographical maps, with the constraint that adjacent cities cannot share the same color, represent a graph coloring problem. Using four colors is sufficient for coloring such maps.

Huffman Codes:

Huffman coding, a lossless data compression algorithm, aims to provide variable-length codes for input characters. The lengths of codes depend on character frequencies, with more frequent characters receiving shorter codes. The coding process ensures that each code assigned to a character is a prefix code, eliminating decoding ambiguities.

Coding Process:

1. **Building a Huffman Tree:**

- For each unique character, a leaf node is created, forming a min-heap.
- The two nodes with the smallest frequencies are extracted and replaced with a new internal node whose frequency is the sum of the extracted nodes. This process repeats until a

single node remains, forming the root of the Huffman tree.

1. **Traversing the Huffman Tree:**

- As the tree is traversed, codes are assigned to characters based on the path taken. Left and right movements correspond to binary digits (0 and 1).

Example: Given character frequencies:
Character | Frequency
a | 5
b | 9
c | 12
d | 13
e | 16
f | 45

The step-by-step process involves creating internal nodes, combining frequencies, and building the Huffman tree. The algorithm stops when only one node remains in the heap.

This method ensures efficient variable-length coding, minimizing the overall bitstream length.

Printing the Codes from the Huffman Tree

To print the codes from the Huffman Tree, you must traverse the tree, starting from the root, while maintaining an auxiliary array. As you navigate to the left child, you append 0 to the array, and for the right child, you append 1. When reaching a leaf node, the array is printed. The C implementation of this approach includes code snippets for creating a Huffman tree and printing the corresponding codes.

GREEDY ALGORITHMS

```c
// C program for Huffman Coding
#include
#include

// Structure for a Huffman tree node
struct MinHeapNode {
char data;
unsigned freq;
struct MinHeapNode* left, *right;
};

// Structure for a Min Heap (or Huffman tree)
struct MinHeap {
unsigned size;
unsigned capacity;
struct MinHeapNode** array;
};

// Function to print codes from the root of the Huffman Tree
void printCodes(struct MinHeapNode* root, int arr[], int top)
{
    if (root->left) {
    arr[top] = 0;
    printCodes(root->left, arr, top + 1);
    }
    if (root->right) {
    arr[top] = 1;
    printCodes(root->right, arr, top + 1);
    }
    if (!(root->left) && !(root->right)) {
    printf("%c: ", root->data);
```

```
    for (int i = 0; i < top; ++i)
    printf("%d", arr[i]);
    printf("\n");
    }
}
```

```
// Main function to build a Huffman Tree and print the codes
    void HuffmanCodes(char data[], int freq[], int size) {
    struct MinHeapNode* root = buildHuffmanTree(data, freq, size);
    int arr[MAX_TREE_HT], top = 0;
    printCodes(root, arr, top);
    }
```

```
// Driver code
    int main() {
    char arr[] = { 'a', 'b', 'c', 'd', 'e', 'f' };
    int freq[] = { 5, 9, 12, 13, 16, 45 };
    int size = sizeof(arr) / sizeof(arr[0]);
    HuffmanCodes(arr, freq, size);
    return 0;
    }
```

This approach has a time complexity of O(n log n), where n is the number of unique characters. The complexity arises from the construction of the Huffman tree, particularly the extractMin() function, which has a time complexity of O(log n) due to the minHeapify() function. Overall, the time complexity of the Huffman codes generation is O(n log n).

Utilizations

The primary application of the Huffman coding algorithm is in scenarios where characters occur consecutively with high frequency. Additionally, it finds widespread use in the transmission of texts and faxes, as well as in compression formats like GZIP and PKZIP, among others.

In the subsequent chapter, we will delve into another method of design known as Dynamic Programming.

5

Dynamic Programming

Dynamic programming is a sophisticated approach wherein we tackle an optimization issue by dividing it into smaller, manageable subproblems and storing the solution to each subproblem. This method ensures that we only solve each subproblem once, enhancing efficiency. While it might seem confusing initially, its effectiveness becomes apparent once you witness it in action. Dynamic programming proves particularly beneficial for optimization problems where finding a minimum or maximum solution within specified constraints is necessary. By thoroughly examining all potential subproblems and avoiding recomputation of solutions, dynamic programming ensures both efficiency and correctness, a feature lacking in many other algorithm-solving techniques.

Initially, it's essential to grasp the concept of subproblems and recognize why memorizing their solutions, known as memoization, holds significance in dynamic programming.

Subproblems

Subproblems, essentially smaller versions of the main problem, closely resemble the primary problem but are often expressed differently. When formulated correctly, a subproblem builds upon other subproblems to contribute to the overall solution.

To illustrate, consider a scenario from the 1950s involving an IBM-650 computer and punch cards. The task is to schedule the processing of these cards efficiently, maximizing their total value. A subproblem in this context might involve determining the optimal schedule for processing a subset of punch cards, sorted by start time.

Subproblems play a crucial role in breaking down the main problem into manageable components, facilitating the solution-building process. Each solved subproblem's solution must be stored or memoized to efficiently address dynamic programming challenges.

Memoization with Fibonacci Numbers

Memoization is a valuable technique when implementing an algorithm to compute Fibonacci numbers for a given input. Traditionally, a recursive algorithm is often chosen, such as this Python example:

```
def fibonacciVal(n):
if n == 0:
return 0
elif n == 1:
return 1
```

else:
return fibonacciVal(n-1) + fibonacciVal(n-2)

While functional, this approach incurs a substantial computational cost. To illustrate, consider the tree of computations needed to determine F(5), where redundant calculations for the subproblem of n=2 occur three times, resulting in unnecessary computation.

Memoization provides a more efficient alternative by calculating the value once, storing it, and accessing it for subsequent instances of the same subproblem. In a dynamic programming implementation, the solution is expressed as follows:

def fibonacciVal(n):
memo = [0] * (n+1)
memo[0], memo[1] = 0, 1
for i in range(2, n+1):
memo[i] = memo[i-1] + memo[i-2]
return memo[n]

In this version, the return value relies on the memo[] array, populated iteratively by the for loop. The iterative filling of memo[] ensures that each subproblem's solution can be derived using previously stored values from already solved subproblems. This eliminates the need to recalculate solutions, resulting in a more efficient algorithm. Memorization is crucial in dynamic programming, ensuring comprehensive consideration of all possibilities before selecting a solution. With this understanding, we can delve deeper into the realm of dynamic programming.

Dynamic Programming Process

The dynamic programming process involves a series of steps, each of which is outlined below.

Step One – Define the Subproblem in Words:

Prior to diving into code, it is crucial to conceptualize the problem at hand. Rather than hastily writing code, take the time to articulate the subproblem using descriptive language. For problems suitable for dynamic programming, identify what needs to be solved and articulate it in terms of subproblems. Consider the punch card problem as an example, where defining the subproblem involves determining the maximum value schedule for punch cards from i to n, sorted by start time. Recognize that this subproblem relies on solving other subproblems.

Step Two – Express Subproblem Mathematically:

Translate the verbalized subproblem into a recurring mathematical decision. This step aids in the coding process and serves as a means to validate the clarity of the defined subproblem. Address two fundamental questions: 1) What decision is needed at each step? 2) Given the algorithm is at step i, what information is required to determine the course of action in i+1? Utilizing the punch card problem as an example, establish a recurrence for the problem, such as $OPT(i) = \max(v\_i + OPT(next[i]), OPT(i+1))$.

Step Three – Utilize Steps One and Two to Solve the Main Problem:

Combine the insights gained from step one, where the subproblem was articulated, and step two, where the mathematical decision was formulated. The primary problem's solution can be expressed as OPT(1), building upon the subproblem structure. Thus, the solution to the main problem mirrors the subproblem, albeit with punch cards numbered from 1 to n.

Step Four – Determine Memoization Array Dimensions and Filling Direction:

Although seemingly counterintuitive, OPT(1) may depend on solutions like OPT(2). This reliance is not problematic if the memoization table is filled in the correct order, similar to the Fibonacci memoization example. Identify the optimal way to fill the table by recognizing dependencies, such as OPT(1) relying on OPT(2) and OPT(next[1]). Determine the memoization array's dimensions based on the variables on which OPT(.) relies. For the punch card problem, a one-dimensional array of size n suffices.

Step Five – Code the Solution:

Integrate steps two through four to craft the dynamic programming code. Combine the mathematical decision, memoization array initialization, and base case to construct an efficient algorithm. As an illustration, consider the dynamic program for the punch card problem, encompassing array initialization, base case setting, and table building.

This comprehensive process equips you to navigate the intricacies of dynamic programming, providing a robust framework for problem-solving and coding.

Paradox of Choice: Dynamic Programming with Multiple Options

While our previous punch card problem involved deciding between two options – to run or not to run a punch card – numerous problems present various choices at each step before reaching a decision. Let's explore a new example.

Imagine you're selling friendship bracelets to n customers, with product values increasing monotonically. The prices $\{p\_1, ..., p\_n\}$ change in a way that if customer j follows customer i, then $p\_i < p\_j$. Their corresponding values are $\{v\_1, ..., v\_n\}$. A customer, i, purchases a bracelet at a price, p_i, ONLY IF $p\_i < v\_i$. Otherwise, the revenue from that specific customer is 0. Assume all prices are natural numbers.

Problem: Find the set of prices that ensures the maximum possible revenue from sales.

Before delving into the steps, ponder how this could be approached.

Step One – Define the Subproblem in Words:

Subproblem – Determine the maximum revenue from customers i to n, where the price for customer i-1 was set at q. Identifying this subproblem involves recognizing the need for answers to subproblems such as the maximum revenue from customers n-2 to n, where n-2 customer's price was q, and so forth. Introducing the new variable, q, ensures monotonic set prices and tracks the current customer through variable i.

Step Two – Express Subproblem Mathematically:

To formulate a recurring mathematical decision, consider two essential questions: 1) What decision is needed at each step? 2) At step i, what information is required to determine what should be done in i+1? For our friendship bracelet problem:
 - Decision at each step: Determine the bracelet's price for the current customer in the range from q to v_i.
 - Information needed at step i+1: Know customer i's set price and customer i+1's value.

The recurrence is expressed as OPT(i, q) = max~([Revenue(v_i, a) + OPT(i+1, a)]), where max~ finds the overall maximum a in the range of q < a < v_i. This recurrence ensures optimal pricing for customer i within the specified range.

The remaining steps follow a similar structure, building upon the foundational understanding established in the first two steps. Go through the subsequent steps outlined in the initial problem to solidify comprehension.

Runtime Analysis of Dynamic Programs

Analyzing the runtime of algorithms adds an exciting dimension to the process of writing them. In this context, we employ big-O notation, a mathematical language that characterizes a function's behavior as its argument approaches infinity or a specific value. This notation proves instrumental in classifying algorithms based on how their space requirements and/or runtime exhibit exponential growth concerning input size.

Typically, the runtime for a dynamic program comprises distinct components:

1. **Pre-processing**: Involves building the memoization array, contributing O(n) to the overall runtime.
2. **The number of times the for loop runs**: Represented as O(n), where 'n' denotes the input size.
3. **Recurrence runtime within the for loop iteration**: The recurrence's runtime is constant (O(1)) since it consistently decides between two options at each iteration.
4. **Post-processing**: No significant processing involved, contributing O(1) to the overall runtime.

The general form for the overall runtime can be expressed as:
$$ \text{Pre-processing} + \text{Loop} \times \text{Recurrence} + \text{Post-processing} $$

To illustrate how big-O notation functions in a dynamic program, let's conduct a runtime analysis using the punch card problem as an example. The provided program focuses on building the memoization array, setting the base case, and iterating through the array to find the solution. The breakdown of runtime components is as follows:

- **Pre-processing**: Building the memoization array (O(n)).
  - **The number of times the for loop runs**: O(n).
  - **Recurrence runtime**:Constant time (O(1)).
  - **Post-processing**:No significant processing (O(1)).

Hence, the overall runtime for this particular problem is represented as $O(n) \times O(n) \times O(1) + O(1)$, which simplifies to $O(n)$.

Dynamic Programming Algorithms

In the realm of dynamic algorithms, we'll delve into two specific ones here – Floyd-Warshall and Bellman-Ford, both falling under the category of All Pair Shortest Path Algorithms.

Floyd-Warshall Algorithm

The Floyd-Warshall algorithm serves the purpose of identifying the shortest path in a weighted graph among all pairs of vertices. Applicable to both undirected and directed weighted graphs, it comes with a caveat – it doesn't function correctly for graphs harboring negative cycles, where the sum of edges in a cycle is negative.

In the context of weighted graphs, where each edge carries a numerical value, the Floyd-Warshall algorithm, also known as Roy-Floyd, Floyd's algorithm, WFI algorithm, or Roy-Warshall algorithm, employs dynamic programming techniques to determine the shortest paths.

How It Works:

1. **Self-loops and parallel edges removal:** Eliminate self-loops and parallel edges while retaining the edge with the lowest weight.
2. **Initial distance matrix creation:** Formulate an initial matrix, denoted as D_0, representing distances between each pair of vertices. Diagonal elements signify self-loops (distance = 0), while non-connected vertices have a distance value of ∞.
3. **Floyd-Warshall iterations:** Develop matrices D_1, D_2, D_3, and D_4 through successive iterations. The final matrix, D_4, encapsulates the shortest distance paths between every pair of vertices.

Implementation:

n = number of vertices
A = n x n matrix

for k = 1 to n
  for i = 1 to n
  for j = 1 to n
  A[i, j] = min(A[k-1, j], A[i, k-1] + A[k-1, j])

return A

The C++ implementation example showcases the practical application of the Floyd-Warshall algorithm on a graph with four vertices.

Time Complexity:

The algorithm's time complexity is $O(n^3)$, where 'n' signifies the number of nodes in the graph. This stems from three nested loops, with the innermost loop involving constant complexity operations.

The Floyd-Warshall algorithm stands as a powerful tool for determining shortest paths, provided the graph adheres to its specific constraints.

Advantages of Floyd-Warshall Algorithm

The Floyd-Warshall algorithm stands out as a powerful tool for determining the shortest path in a weighted graph, accommodating both negative and positive edge weights. Executing the algorithm once provides the shortest path length between all pairs of vertices. Its versatility extends to easy modification for path reconstruction, finding a transitive closure of a relation R, and identifying the widest path in a weighted graph.

Disadvantages of Floyd-Warshall

However, the algorithm has limitations. It can only ascertain the shortest path in the absence of negative cycles in the graph and does not furnish path details.

Applications

The Floyd-Warshall algorithm finds applications in various

scenarios:

- Discovering the shortest path in directed weighted graphs
- Determining the transitive closure in directed weighted graphs
- Real matrix inversion
- Verifying if an undirected graph is bipartite.

Bellman-Ford Algorithm

The Bellman-Ford algorithm, another contender for finding the shortest path in weighted graphs, caters to scenarios where there may be negative weight edges. While Dijkstra's algorithm is an alternative, it operates on a greedy approach and doesn't handle graphs with negative weight cycles.

Algorithm Steps:

1. **Initialization:** Set distances as infinite between the source vertex (src) and all other vertices. Create an array **dist[]** with all values set as infinite, except **dist[src]**, which is set to 0.
2. **Shortest Distance Calculation:** Repeat the following steps |V| - 1 times (where |V| is the number of vertices):

- For each edge u-v, update **dist[v]** if **dist[v] > dist[u] + weight of edge uv**.

1. **Negative Cycle Check:** If, after the above steps, there is still a shorter path for any vertex, it indicates the presence of a negative weight cycle in the graph.

The Bellman-Ford algorithm employs a dynamic programming approach, iteratively calculating the shortest distances for paths with an increasing number of edges. The outer loop ensures this calculation for paths with up to |V| - 1 edges.

An illustrative example graph, with source vertex 0 and five vertices, aids in understanding the algorithm's workings. The distances are initialized, and all edges are processed four times, corresponding to the number of vertices minus one.

The edges are sequentially processed as follows: (B, E), (D, B), (B, D), (A, B), (A, C), (D, C), (B, C), (E, D). The initial distances are depicted in the first row, while the second row showcases distances after processing edges (B, E), (D, B), and (A, B). Subsequently, the third row illustrates distances from (A, C), and the final row presents distances for (D, C), (B, C), and (D, E). The first iteration ensures the shortest distances for paths with no more than one edge. After the second iteration, distances for paths with no more than two edges are guaranteed. Further iterations minimize distances, and after the third and fourth iterations, no updates occur.

The C++ implementation of the Bellman-Ford algorithm is provided below:

```
// A C++ program for Bellman-Ford's single source
// shortest path algorithm.
#include
// The structure represents a weighted edge in the graph
struct Edge {
int src, dest, weight;
};
// The structure represents a connected, directed and
// weighted graph
```

```
struct Graph {
// V-> Number of vertices, E-> Number of edges
int V, E;
// The graph is represented as an array of edges.
struct Edge* edge;
};
// This creates a graph with V vertices and E edges
struct Graph* createGraph(int V, int E)
{
struct Graph* graph = new Graph;
graph->V = V;
graph->E = E;
graph->edge = new Edge[E];
return graph;
}
// A utility function used to print the solution
void printArr(int dist[], int n)
{
printf("Vertex Distance from Source\n");
for (int i = 0; i < n; ++i)
printf("%d \t\t %d\n", i, dist[i]);
}
// The main function used to find the shortest distances from src to
// all other vertices using the Bellman-Ford algorithm. The function
// also detects a negative weight cycle in the graph
void BellmanFord(struct Graph* graph, int src)
{
int V = graph->V;
int E = graph->E;
```

```c
int dist[V];
// Step 1: Initialize the distances from src to all other vertices
// as INFINITE
for (int i = 0; i < V; i++)
dist[i] = INT_MAX;
dist[src] = 0;
// Step 2: Relax all the edges |V| - 1 times. A simple shortest
// path from src to any other vertex can have at-most |V| - 1
// edges
for (int i = 1; i <= V - 1; i++) {
for (int j = 0; j < E; j++) {
int u = graph->edge[j].src;
int v = graph->edge[j].dest;
int weight = graph->edge[j].weight;
if (dist[u] != INT_MAX && dist[u] + weight < dist[v])
dist[v] = dist[u] + weight;
}
}
// Step 3: check for negative-weight cycles. The above step
// guarantees the shortest distances if the graph doesn't contain
// a negative weight cycle. If we get a shorter path, then there
// is a negative weight cycle.
for (int i = 0; i < E; i++) {
int u = graph->edge[i].src;
int v = graph->edge[i].dest;
int weight = graph->edge[i].weight;
if (dist[u] != INT_MAX && dist[u] + weight < dist[v]) {
printf("contains a negative weight cycle");
return; // If a negative cycle is detected, simply return
}
```

```
}
printArr(dist, V);
return;
}
// Driver program to test above functions
int main()
{
/* Let us create the graph given in the above example */
int V = 5; // Number of vertices in graph
int E = 8; // Number of edges in graph
struct Graph* graph = createGraph(V, E);
// add edge 0-1 (or A-B in above figure)
graph->edge[0].src = 0;
graph->edge[0].dest = 1;
graph->edge[0].weight = -1;
// add edge 0-2 (or A-C in above figure)
graph->edge[1].src = 0;
graph->edge[1].dest = 2;
graph->edge[1].weight = 4;
// add edge 1-2 (or B-C in above figure)
graph->edge[2].src = 1;
graph->edge[2].dest = 2;
graph->edge[2].weight = 3;
// add edge 1-3 (or B-D in above figure)
graph->edge[3].src = 1;
graph->edge[3].dest = 3;
graph->edge[3].weight = 2;
// add edge 1-4 (or A-E in above figure)
graph->edge[4].src = 1;
graph->edge[4].dest = 4;
graph->edge[4].weight = 2;
```

```cpp
// add edge 3-2 (or D-C in above figure)
graph->edge[5].src = 3;
graph->edge[5].dest = 2;
graph->edge[5].weight = 5;
// add edge 3-1 (or D-B in above figure)
graph->edge[6].src = 3;
graph->edge[6].dest = 1;
graph->edge[6].weight = 1;
// add edge 4-3 (or E-D in above figure)
graph->edge[7].src = 4;
graph->edge[7].dest = 3;
graph->edge[7].weight = -3;
BellmanFord(graph, 0);
return 0;
}
```

The edges are sequentially processed as follows: (B, E), (D, B), (B, D), (A, B), (A, C), (D, C), (B, C), (E, D). The initial distances are depicted in the first row, while the second row showcases distances after processing edges (B, E), (D, B), and (A, B). Subsequently, the third row illustrates distances from (A, C), and the final row presents distances for (D, C), (B, C), and (D, E). The first iteration ensures the shortest distances for paths with no more than one edge. After the second iteration, distances for paths with no more than two edges are guaranteed. Further iterations minimize distances, and after the third and fourth iterations, no updates occur.

Implementation:

The C++ implementation of the Bellman-Ford algorithm is provided below:

```cpp
// A C++ program for Bellman-Ford's single source
// shortest path algorithm.
#include <bits/stdc++.h>
// The structure represents a weighted edge in the
graph
struct Edge {
    int src, dest, weight;
};
// The structure represents a connected, directed and
// weighted graph
struct Graph {
    // V-> Number of vertices, E-> Number of edges
    int V, E;
    // The graph is represented as an array of edges.
    struct Edge* edge;
};
// This creates a graph with V vertices and E edges
struct Graph* createGraph(int V, int E)
{
    struct Graph* graph = new Graph;
    graph->V = V;
    graph->E = E;
    graph->edge = new Edge[E];
    return graph;
}
// A utility function used to print the solution
void printArr(int dist[], int n)
{
    printf("Vertex   Distance from Source\n");
    for (int i = 0; i < n; ++i)
        printf("%d \t\t %d\n", i, dist[i]);
}
// The main function used to find the shortest
distances from src to
// all other vertices using the Bellman-Ford
algorithm. The function
```

```c
// also detects a negative weight cycle in the graph
void BellmanFord(struct Graph* graph, int src)
{
    int V = graph->V;
    int E = graph->E;
    int dist[V];
    // Step 1: Initialize the distances from src to all other vertices
    // as INFINITE
    for (int i = 0; i < V; i++)
        dist[i] = INT_MAX;
    dist[src] = 0;
    // Step 2: Relax all the edges |V| - 1 times. A simple shortest
    // path from src to any other vertex can have at-most |V| - 1
    // edges
    for (int i = 1; i <= V - 1; i++) {
        for (int j = 0; j < E; j++) {
            int u = graph->edge[j].src;
            int v = graph->edge[j].dest;
            int weight = graph->edge[j].weight;
            if (dist[u] != INT_MAX && dist[u] +
            weight < dist[v])
                dist[v] = dist[u] + weight;
        }
    }
    // Step 3: check for negative-weight cycles.  The above step
    // guarantees the shortest distances if the graph doesn't contain
    // a negative weight cycle.  If we get a shorter path, then there
    // is a negative weight cycle.
    for (int i = 0; i < E; i++) {
        int u = graph->edge[i].src;
        int v = graph->edge[i].dest;
```

DYNAMIC PROGRAMMING

```
            int weight = graph->edge[i].weight;
            if (dist[u] != INT_MAX && dist[u] + weight <
            dist[v]) {
                printf("contains a negative weight
                cycle");
                return; // If a negative cycle is
                detected, simply return
            }
        }
        printArr(dist, V);
        return;
}
// Driver program to test above functions
int main()
{
        /* Let us create the graph given in the above
        example */
        int V = 5; // Number of vertices in graph
        int E = 8; // Number of edges in graph
        struct Graph* graph = createGraph(V, E);
        // add edge 0-1 (or A-B in above figure)
        graph->edge[0].src = 0;
        graph->edge[0].dest = 1;
        graph->edge[0].weight = -1;
        // add edge 0-2 (or A-C in above figure)
        graph->edge[1].src = 0;
        graph->edge[1].dest = 2;
        graph->edge[1].weight = 4;
        // add edge 1-2 (or B-C in above figure)
        graph->edge[2].src = 1;
        graph->edge[2].dest = 2;
        graph->edge[2].weight = 3;
        // add edge 1-3 (or B-D in above figure)
        graph->edge[3].src = 1;
        graph->edge[3].dest = 3;
        graph->edge[3].weight = 2;
        // add edge 1-4 (or A-E in above figure)
```

```
        graph->edge[4].src = 1;
        graph->edge[4].dest = 4;
        graph->edge[4].weight = 2;
        // add edge 3-2 (or D-C in above figure)
        graph->edge[5].src = 3;
        graph->edge[5].dest = 2;
        graph->edge[5].weight = 5;
        // add edge 3-1 (or D-B in above figure)
        graph->edge[6].src = 3;
        graph->edge[6].dest = 1;
        graph->edge[6].weight = 1;
        // add edge 4-3 (or E-D in above figure)
        graph->edge[7].src = 4;
        graph->edge[7].dest = 3;
        graph->edge[7].weight = -3;
        BellmanFord(graph, 0);
        return 0;
}
```

Output:

Vertex Distance from Source 0 0 1 -1 2 2 3 -2 4 1

Note:

1. Negative cycles are common in various graph applications, where choosing a path might be more advantageous than incurring a cost.
2. The Bellman-Ford algorithm is preferred over alternatives, such as Dijkstra's, for distributed systems. Unlike Dijkstra's, which requires finding the minimum value for every vertex, Bellman-Ford considers each edge individually.
3. Bellman-Ford is not suitable for undirected graphs with negative edges, as they are deemed to contain negative

cycles.

This concludes our exploration of dynamic programming techniques, paving the way for the branch and bound technique.

6

Branch and Bound

The branch and bound methodology is a common design approach employed to address problems characterized by combinatorial optimization. Such problems often exhibit exponential time complexity, requiring exploration of every possible permutation in worst-case scenarios. Branch and bound provides an efficient solution to rapidly solve these types of problems.

To illustrate the application of branch and bound, let's examine the 0/1 knapsack problem. Various algorithms can solve this problem, including dynamic programming for 0/1 knapsack, the greedy algorithm for fractional knapsack, and a backtracking solution for 0/1 knapsack. Specifically, we'll focus on Knapsack Using Branch and Bound.

Consider a scenario with two integer arrays, val[0...n-1] and wt[0...n-1], representing values and weights for n items. The objective is to identify the maximum value subset of val[] while ensuring that the sum of weights in the subset is equal to or less than the knapsack capacity, denoted as W.

Several approaches can be employed to address this problem:

1. Greedy Approach:
This method selects items in decreasing order of value-per-unit weight. While effective for fractional knapsack problems, it may not yield accurate results for 0/1 knapsack.

2. Dynamic Programming:
Utilizing a 2D table with dimensions n x W, this approach is suitable when item weights are integers.

3. Brute Force:
Though not always efficient, a brute force solution involves generating 2^n solutions for n items. Each solution is checked to ensure it meets the constraints, and the maximum satisfying solution is retained. This solution can be visualized as a tree.

To optimize the brute force solution, backtracking can be applied. By conducting a depth-first search on the tree, the algorithm can terminate exploration at points where a feasible solution is no longer viable. In the presented example, backtracking proves more effective when the knapsack capacity is smaller or when dealing with a larger number of items.

Branch and Bound:

To enhance the backtracking solution, we can optimize it by determining a bound on the best possible subtree rooted with all nodes. The node and subtrees can be disregarded if the subtree's best is inferior to the current best. The best solution (bound) is calculated for each node and compared with the current bound before exploring the node.

In the example bounds are as follows:
- A down – capable of providing $315
- B down – capable of providing $275
- C down – capable of providing $225
- D down – capable of providing $125
- E down - can provide $30

We will discuss how to obtain these bounds shortly. While the branch and bounds technique is valuable for searching for a solution, the entire tree must be fully calculated in the worst-case scenario. In the best-case scenario, only one path needs complete calculation through the tree, while the remaining paths can be pruned.

Implementation:

The implementation of the 0/1 knapsack problem using the branch and bound technique is presented. After evaluating various techniques, it was determined that branch and bound is most effective when item weights are not integers. The goal is to find the bound for all nodes in the 0/1 knapsack problem, leveraging the fact that the greedy approach works well for the fractional knapsack problem.

The optimal solution is derived through the node, employing the greedy approach to determine if a specific node offers a superior solution. If the solution surpasses the current best, there is no possibility of obtaining a better solution through the node.

The algorithm follows these steps:

1. Sort all items in decreasing order of the value-to-weight ratio to compute the upper bound using the greedy approach.
2. Initialize the maximum profit (maxProfit) to 0.
3. Create an empty queue (Q).
4. Generate a dummy node of the decision tree with a profit and weight of 0, enqueuing it to Q.
5. While Q is not empty, perform the following:

a. Extract an item (u) from Q.

b. Compute the profit of the next-level node. If it exceeds maxProfit, update maxProfit.

c. Calculate the bound of the next-level node. If it surpasses maxProfit, add the next-level node to Q.

d. Consider a scenario where the next-level node is excluded from the solution – add a node to the queue with the level set as the next level but without considering the weight and profit.

Illustration: Example Input: // Each pair consists of the weight and value of the item Item arr[] = {{2, 40}, {3.14, 50}, {1.98, 100}, {5,

95}, {3, 30}}; Knapsack Capacity W = 10 Result: The maximum achievable profit = 235

This can be visualized in the diagram below, depicting the items sorted by value/weight.

Please note that the image does not strictly adhere to the algorithm due to the absence of a dummy node, but it provides a conceptual understanding. Additionally, a C++ implementation of the above is presented:

// C++ program to solve knapsack problem using // branch and bound #include <bits/stdc++.h> using namespace std;

// The structure for the Item storing the weight and corresponding // value of the Item struct Item { float weight; int value; };

// Node structure storing information of the decision tree struct Node { // level —> Level of the node in the decision tree (or index // in arr[]) // profit —> Profit of the nodes on the path from the root to this // node (including this node) // bound —-> The upper bound of the maximum profit in the subtree // of this node/ int level, profit, bound; float weight; };

// A comparison function to sort Item based on // val/weight ratio bool cmp(Item a, Item b) { double r1 = (double)a.value / a.weight; double r2 = (double)b.value / b.weight; return r1 > r2; }

// Returns the bound of profit in the subtree rooted with u. // This function mainly uses the Greedy solution to find // an upper bound on maximum profit. int bound(Node u, int n, int W, Item arr[]) { // If weight surpasses the knapsack capacity, return // 0 as the expected bound if (u.weight >= W) return 0;

// Initialize the bound on profit with the current profit
    int profit_bound = u.profit;

```
// Start including items from an index 1 more than the current
// item index
int j = u.level + 1;
int totweight = u.weight;

// Check the index condition and knapsack capacity
// condition
while ((j < n) && (totweight + arr[j].weight <= W))
{
    totweight += arr[j].weight;
    profit_bound += arr[j].value;
    j++;
}

// If j is not n, include the last item partially for
// an upper bound on profit
if (j < n)
    profit_bound += (W - totweight) * arr[j].value /
    arr[j].weight;

return profit_bound;
}
// Returns the maximum profit we can get with capacity W
int knapsack(int W, Item arr[], int n) { // Sort items based on
the value per unit // weight. sort(arr, arr + n, cmp);
    // Create a queue for traversing the nodes
    queue Q;
    Node u, v;

    // Dummy node at the beginning
    u.level = -1;
```

```
    u.profit = u.weight = 0;
    Q.push(u);

// Extract the items one by one from the decision tree
    // and compute the profit of all children of the extracted item
    // and keep saving maxProfit
    int maxProfit = 0;

while (!Q.empty())
    {
    // Dequeue a node
    u = Q.front();
    Q.pop();

// If it is the starting node, assign level 0
    if (u.level == -1)
    v.level = 0;

// If there is nothing on the next level
    if (u.level == n - 1)
    continue;

// Else if not the last node, then increment level,
    // and compute the profit of children nodes.
    v.level = u.level + 1;

// Take the current level's item and add the current
    // level's weight and value to node u's
    // weight and value
    v.weight = u.weight + arr[v.level].weight;
    v.profit = u.profit + arr[v.level].value;
```

```
  // If the cumulated weight is less than W and
     // profit is greater than the previous profit,
     // update maxProfit
     if (v.weight <= W && v.profit > maxProfit)
     maxProfit = v.profit;

  // Get the upper bound on profit to decide
     // whether to add v to Q or not.
     v.bound = bound(v, n, W, arr);

  // If the bound value is greater than profit,
     // then only push into the queue for further
     // consideration
     if (v.bound > maxProfit)
     Q.push(v);

  // Do the same thing, but without taking
     // the item in the knapsack
     v.weight = u.weight;
     v.profit = u.profit;
     v.bound = bound(v, n, W, arr);

  if (v.bound > maxProfit)
     Q.push(v);
     }

  return maxProfit;
     }
     // Driver program to test the above function int main() { int
  W = 10; // Weight of the knapsack Item arr[] = {{2, 40}, {3.14, 50},
  {1.98, 100}, {5, 95}, {3, 30}}; int n = sizeof(arr) / sizeof(arr[0]); cout
```

« "Maximum possible profit = " « knapsack(W, arr, n); return 0;
}

Output: Maximum possible profit = 235

Utilizing Branch and Bound for Generating Binary Strings of Length N

Examples: Given input N, the desired output is: 000 001 010 011 100 101 110 111

Explanation: For binary digits of length three, the corresponding numbers are 0, 1, 2, 3, 4, 5, 6, 7.

Another example is given by input N and output: 00 01 10 11

Approach: Employing branch and bound to generate combinations involves initializing an empty solution vector. While the queue is not empty, a partial vector is removed from the queue. If this vector is the last one, the combination is printed. Otherwise, for the next partial vector component, k child vectors are created by fixing all possible states for that component, and these vectors are inserted into the queue.

Here is the implementation of this approach in C++:

```
// CPP Program to generate
// Binary Strings using Branch and Bound
#include
using namespace std;

// Creating a Node class
    class Node
    {
    public:
    int *soln;
```

```
    int level;
    vector child;
    Node(Node *parent, int level, int N)
    {
    this->parent = parent;
    this->level = level;
    this->soln = new int[N];
    }
};

// A utility function to generate the binary strings of length n
    void generate(Node *n, int &N, queue &Q)
    {
    // If the list is full, print combination
    if (n->level == N)
    {
    for (int i = 0; i < N; i++)
    cout « n->soln[i];
    cout « endl;
    }
    else
    {
    int l = n->level;
    // iterate while length is not equal to n
    for (int i = 0; i <= 1; i++)
    {
    Node *x = new Node(n, l + 1, N);
    for (int k = 0; k < l; k++)
    x->soln[k] = n->soln[k];
    x->soln[l] = i;
    n->child.push_back(x);
```

```
        Q.push(x);
    }
  }
}

// Driver Code
  int main()
  {
  // Initiate Generation
  // Create a root Node
  int N = 3;
  Node *root;
  root = new Node(NULL, 0, N);
  // Queue that maintains the list of live Nodes
  queue Q;
  // Instantiate the Queue
  Q.push(root);
  while (!Q.empty())
  {
  Node *E = Q.front();
  Q.pop();
  generate(E, N, Q);
  }
  return 0;
  }
  Output: 000 001 010 011 100 101 110 111
```
This approach has a time complexity of $O(2^n)$.

7

Randomized Algorithm

A randomized algorithm incorporates random numbers in its decision-making process. For instance, in the randomized Quicksort algorithm, the choice of the next pivot or the random shuffling of an array involves the use of random numbers. This randomness is employed to mitigate time or space complexity in conventional algorithms.

Let's delve into the workings of conditional probability:
Conditional probability, denoted as P(A | B), signifies the probability of event A occurring given that event B has already taken place.
$$ P(A | B) = \frac{P(A \cap B)}{P(B)} $$

The interrelation between P(A | B) and P(B | A) is elucidated through Bayes' conditional probability formula.

Examining the conditional probability formulas P(A | B) and P(B | A):
$$ P(A | B) = - - - 1 $$

DESIGN ALGORITHMS TO SOLVE COMMON PROBLEMS

$$P(B \mid A) = ---2$$

By substituting $P(B \cap A) = P(A \cap B)$, the first formula can be expressed as $P(A \mid B) = \frac{P(B \mid A)P(A)}{P(B)}$.

Random variables, which map random event outcomes to real values, are integral to understanding probability. Consider a coin-tossing game where a player gains $50 for "Heads" and loses $50 for "Tails." The random variable profit can be defined as:

$$\text{Profit} = \begin{cases} +50 & \text{if Heads} \\ -50 & \text{if Tails} \end{cases}$$

Expected value (E[R]) for a random variable is computed as the sum of the product of the probability and the value of the variable for every possible event.

$$E[R] = r_1 \cdot p_1 + r_2 \cdot p_2 + \ldots + r_k \cdot p_k$$

The linearity of expectation asserts that the expected value of the sum of two random variables is the sum of their individual expected values.

For instance, considering three dice throws with an expected value of $3 \cdot \frac{7}{2} = 7$ illustrates the linearity of expectation.

Determining the expected number of trials until success involves considering the probability of success (p). For instance, if a 6-faced die is thrown until a 5 appears, the expected number of trials is $1/p = 6$.

In the context of a Quicksort version choosing pivots until one of the n/2 elements in the middle is selected, the expected number of trials is 2, given that the probability of choosing one of the n/2 middle elements is $\frac{1}{2}$.

Analyzing Randomized Algorithms

Some randomized algorithms exhibit deterministic time complexity, known as Monte Carlo algorithms, making their worst-case analysis relatively straightforward. In contrast, Las Vegas algorithms' time complexity depends on a random variable's value, requiring analysis in terms of the expected worst-case scenario. To calculate the expected time in the worst case, every potential value of the random variable must be considered, along with the time taken for each value. The average of these times represents the time complexity for the worst case.

Consider the example of a randomized quicksort algorithm with central pivots dividing arrays to ensure one side has at least 1/4 of the elements. The key observation is that the second step, involving a while loop, has a time complexity of O(n).

How many iterations does the while loop need to find a central pivot? There is a 1/n probability that the randomly chosen element is a central pivot, implying an expected loop runtime of n times. Consequently, the expected time complexity for step two is O(n).

In the worst case, the array is partitioned to have n/4 elements on one side and 3n/4 on the other. The recursion tree's height in the worst-case scenario is Log 3/4nm, resulting in O(Log n).

\[T(n) < T(n/4) + T(3n/4) + O(n) \]

\[T(n) < 2T(3n/4) + O(n) \]

The recurrence relation's solution is O(Log n).

It's essential to note that the aforementioned randomized quicksort algorithm isn't the optimal approach. This analysis aims for simplicity. Typically, a more sophisticated implementation involves randomly choosing a pivot without a loop or shuffling array elements. This alternative algorithm has an expected time complexity of O(n Log n), with a more intricate analysis beyond our current scope.

Analyzing Randomized Algorithms: Types, Examples, and Applications

Randomized algorithms are categorized into two main types, briefly discussed earlier:

1. **Las Vegas Algorithms:**

- Always yield an optimal or correct result.
- Time complexity is based on random values, typically evaluated as the expected value.
- Example: Randomized Quicksort, which sorts input arrays

with an O(n log n) time complexity in the worst-case scenario.

1. **Monte Carlo Algorithms:**

- Produce optimal or correct results with a probability degree.
- Have a deterministic running time, making worst-case time complexity analysis more straightforward.
- Example: Karger's algorithm, with some implementations providing a minimum cut probability of $1/n^2$, where n is the number of vertices. Time complexity is O(E).

Understanding the Classification:

Consider a binary array with precisely 50% of its elements as 0 and the rest as 1. The goal is to find the index of any 1. A Las Vegas algorithm randomly chooses elements until it finds a 1. In contrast, a Monte Carlo algorithm selects random elements until it finds a 1 or exhausts the maximum allowable attempts (k). The Las Vegas algorithm always finds a 1, with the expected number of trials being 2, resulting in an O(1) expected time complexity.

The Solovay-Strassen Primality Test:

Primality testers, crucial in cryptography and cybersecurity, determine whether a specified integer is prime. The Solovay-Strassen Primality Test, developed by Volker Strassen and Robert M. Solovay, is a probabilistic test for primality.

Key Concepts:

1. **Legendre Symbol (a/p):**

- Defined on integers a and p.
- Follows Euler's criterion.

1. **Jacobi Symbol (a/n):**

- Generalization of Legendre's symbol.
- Computed based on prime factors.

Algorithm:

1. Choose a number (n) for primality testing and a random number (a) from the (2, n-1) range.
2. Compute the Jacobi symbol (a/n).
3. If n is prime, the Jacobi symbol equals the Legendre symbol, satisfying Euler's criterion.
4. If not, n is considered composite, and the program stops.
5. Accuracy and iterations are directly proportional; multiple runs enhance accuracy.

Solovay-Strassen Primality Test Pseudocode:
```
boolean SolovayStrassen(double p, int k):
if(p < 2):
return false
if(p != 2 and p % 2 == 0):
return false
for(int i = 0; i < k; i++):
double a = rand() % (p - 1) + 1
double jacobian = (p + Jacobi(a, p)) % p
double mod = modExp(a, (p - 1) / 2, p)
if(!jacobian || mod != jacobian)
return false
```

return true

Randomized algorithms leverage randomness to make decisions, offering faster solutions than deterministic approaches. This randomness is prevalent in machine learning applications:

- Randomly initializing algorithm states, such as in artificial neural networks.
- Resolving ties in deterministic methods using randomness.
- Randomly splitting data into training and testing sets.
- Randomly shuffling training datasets in stochastic gradient descent.

Applications and Scope:

Randomized algorithms excel in various applications, including cryptography, load balancing, primality testing, data structures (sorting, hashing, etc.), algebraic identities, counting and enumeration, graph algorithms, parallel and distributed computing, probabilistic existence proofs, and derandomization.

In summary, Monte Carlo algorithms are fast and almost certainly correct, while Las Vegas algorithms are not always fast but consistently correct. These algorithms play a crucial role in diverse fields, showcasing their versatility and efficiency.

8

Recursion and Backtracking

In the concluding chapter, we will delve into the last two methodologies: recursion and backtracking.

Recursion

Recursion is a procedural concept where a function invokes itself either directly or indirectly, and the function identified by this process is termed a recursive function. It finds application in solving specific problems effortlessly, such as the Towers of Hanoi (TOH), Depth-First Search (DFS) of Graphs, and various tree traversals like Inorder, Preorder, and Postorder.

To illustrate recursion, let's examine a scenario where a programmer aims to calculate the sum of the first 'n' natural numbers. The straightforward approach involves adding the numbers from 1 to 'n', which can be expressed as $f(n) = 1 + 2 + 3 + \ldots + n$.

Alternatively, we can adopt a distinct mathematical perspective, wherein the recursive approach is employed:

- Recursive adding approach (f(n) = 1 for n = 1, f(n) = n + f(n-1) for n > 1).

This dichotomy arises from the second approach's inclusion of a function call within itself, termed recursion. This recursive function holds significance for programmers, offering an efficient means to code certain problems.

What is Base Condition?

The concept of a base condition is integral to recursive programming. It involves establishing a solution for the base case within the recursive program, with smaller programs addressing the larger problem's solution. A case in point is the recursive factorial function, defined as:

```
int fact(int n)
{
if (n <= 1) // base case
return 1;
else
return n * fact(n-1);
}
```

In this example, the base case is set as n <= 1, and the function operates by progressively reducing larger values of 'n' until the base case is reached.

Understanding recursion involves viewing a problem as one or more smaller problems, with base conditions halting the recursion. For instance, the computation of the factorial of 'n' relies on knowing the factorial of (n-1), and the base case is n = 0, where the function returns 1.

The issue of stack overflow errors in recursion arises when

a base case is not defined or cannot be reached, leading to a memory exhaustion problem. An erroneous example is provided where the base case is set as n == 100, resulting in stack overflow as the recursive calls do not reach the base case.

Distinguishing between direct and indirect recursion is another aspect to ponder. A function is directly recursive if it calls the same function, whereas it becomes indirectly recursive when it calls a different function, which may further invoke the original function, creating a chain.

Examples are presented for both direct and indirect recursion, showcasing the recursive nature of programming and the potential pitfalls associated with improper base case definitions.

How Memory is Allocated for Function Calls

When a function is called from **main()**, memory is allocated on the stack. In the case of a recursive function calling itself, the memory for the called function is allocated on top of the memory assigned to the calling function. Subsequently, local variables are duplicated, with one set for each function call. Upon reaching the base case, the value is returned from the function to its caller, leading to memory deallocation, and the process continues.

To illustrate this, consider a simple C++ program demonstrating recursion:

```
#include
using namespace std;

void printFun(int test) {
  if (test < 1)
  return;
```

```
else {
cout « test « " ";
printFun(test - 1); // statement 2
cout « test « " ";
return;
}
}

int main() {
  int test = 3;
  printFun(test);
}
```

When **printFun(3)** is called from **main()**, memory is allocated, initializing a local variable **test** to 3, and statements 1 to 4 are pushed onto the stack. The execution starts with printing 3, then **printFun(2)** is called, leading to a sequence of function calls and outputting values from 3 to 1 and then from 1 to 3.

Moving forward, let's explore a practical problem that recursion can solve: finding the Fibonacci sequence for a given 'n' where n > 2. The mathematical equation for Fibonacci is defined as:

- n if n == 0 or n == 1;
- fib(n) = fib(n-1) + fib(n-2) otherwise;

Here is the recursive implementation in C++:
```
#include
using namespace std;

int fib(int n) {
```

```
if (n == 0)
return 0;
if (n == 1 || n == 2)
return 1;
else
return (fib(n - 1) + fib(n - 2));
}

int main() {
    int n = 5;
    cout << "Fibonacci series of 5 numbers is: ";
    for (int i = 0; i < n; i++) {
        cout << fib(i) << " ";
    }
    return 0;
}
```

The recursive tree for input 5 is depicted, showcasing the breakdown of smaller problems to solve the larger one. The time complexity of the Fibonacci function is discussed in terms of function calls, illustrating the dependence on function call complexities. For the best case, the time complexity is denoted as $()=(2/2)T(n)=\vartheta(2n/2)$.

Task 2:

Develop a program and its corresponding recurrence relation to compute the factorial of a given number n where $>2n>2$.

Mathematical Equation: 1 if $=0$ or $=1$; 1 if $n=0$ or $n=1$; $()=\cdot(-1)$ if >1; $f(n)=n\cdot f(n-1)$ if $n>1$;

Recurrence Relation: $()=1$ for $=0$; $T(n)=1$ for $n=0$; $()=1+(-1)$

for >0; $T(n)=1+T(n-1)$ for $n>0$;
Implementation:
```cpp
// C++ program to calculate factorial
#include
using namespace std;

// Factorial function
int factorial(int n) {
// Base case
if (n == 0 || n == 1)
return 1;
// Recursive case
else
return n * factorial(n - 1);
}

// Driver code
int main() {
int n = 5;
cout « "Factorial of " « n « " is: " « factorial(n);
return 0;
}
```
Output:Factorial of 5 is: 120

Advantages and Disadvantages of Recursive Programming vs. Iterative Programming

Recursive and iterative programs share similar capabilities for problem-solving. This means that recursive problems can be written iteratively, and vice versa. Recursive programs demand more space compared to iterative ones because the functions persist in the stack until reaching the base case. Recursive programming also entails greater space requirements due to return overheads and function calls. However, recursion offers a cleaner and more straightforward coding approach.

Certain problems, such as the Tower of Hanoi, tree traversals, and others, inherently lend themselves to recursion, making recursive code preferable for such cases. Additionally, iterative approaches can be employed for these problems using a stack data structure.

Backtracking

Backtracking is a technique employed for recursively solving problems by gradually constructing a solution, addressing one component at a time. Unsatisfactory solutions, those failing to meet the problem's constraints at any stage, are discarded. In this context, "time" refers to the duration until any level of the search tree is reached.

Backtracking encompasses three types of problems:

1. Decision Problems – Seeking feasible solutions
2. Optimization Problems – Aiming for the best solution
3. Enumeration Problems – Identifying every feasible solution

Determining the Applicability of Backtracking:

Backtracking is typically suitable for constraint satisfaction problems characterized by well-defined constraints on an objective solution. Candidates are incrementally built, and backtracking is applied or abandons a candidate once it is evident that the candidate cannot fulfill and provide a valid solution.

While many problems can be solved using greedy or dynamic programming algorithms, which offer linear, logarithmic, or linear-logarithmic time complexity concerning input size, backtracking algorithms often exhibit exponential space and time complexity. Despite this, there are specific problems that only backtracking can effectively address.

Consider the example of three boxes, one containing a gold coin. The objective is to find the coin by opening each box one at a time, eliminating possibilities until the coin is discovered. This exemplifies backtracking's fundamental approach of reaching the optimal solution by solving subproblems sequentially.

Formal Backtracking Algorithm:

Let's consider a computational problem, P, and corresponding data, D, with constraints represented by C. The backtracking algorithm operates as follows:

1. Start building the solution with the empty solution set, S = {}.
2. Add the first left move to S, creating a new subtree, S, in the algorithm's subtree.
3. Ensure S satisfies the three C constraints: a. If yes, the

subtree S can add more children. b. If not, subtree S is deemed useless, and argument S is used to recur back to step one.
4. If the new subtree is eligible to add children, argument S + s is used to recur to step one.
5. If a check for S + s confirms it as the solution for D, the program is output and terminated. If not, it is discarded.

Backtracking vs. Recursion:

Recursion necessitates the function calling itself until the base case is reached. In backtracking, recursion is employed to explore every possibility until the optimal solution is found.

Pseudocode for Backtracking:

1. Recursive backtracking solution.

```
void findSolutions(n, other params) :
  if (found a solution) :
  solutionsFound = solutionsFound + 1;
  displaySolution();
  if (solutionsFound >= solutionTarget) :
  System.exit(0);
  return
  for (val = first to last) :
  if (isValid(val, n)) :
  applyValue(val, n);
  findSolutions(n+1, other params);
  removeValue(val, n);
  Determining if a solution exists
  boolean findSolutions(n, other params) :
```

```
if (found a solution) :
displaySolution();
return true;
for (val = first to last) :
if (isValid(val, n)) :
applyValue(val, n);
if (findSolutions(n+1, other params))
return true;
removeValue(val, n);
return false;
```

The Challenge of the Knight's Tour

We now understand that backtracking is an algorithmic technique to explore various solutions systematically. Typically, problems addressed with this technique follow a consistent approach, trying each potential solution exactly once. A simplistic approach would involve testing all solutions and outputting one that adheres to the specified problem constraints.

Backtracking operates incrementally and serves as a Naïve solution optimization. One intriguing problem that can be tackled using this technique is the Knight's Tour.

Consider a chessboard with dimensions N*N, where the Knight starts on an empty board's initial block. The goal is for the Knight to visit each square precisely once, adhering to the rules of chess, and printing the order in which the squares are visited.

For instance, with N = 8, the output may resemble the following 8*8 matrix:

0 59 38 33 30 17 8 63
37 34 31 60 9 62 29 16
58 1 36 39 32 27 18 7

35 48 41 26 61 10 15 28
42 57 2 49 40 23 6 19
47 50 45 54 25 20 11 14
56 43 52 3 22 13 24 5
51 46 55 44 53 4 21 12

First, let's explore the Naïve algorithm and then delve into the Backtracking approach.

Naïve Algorithm:

The Naïve algorithm generates each tour individually, checking if it satisfies the specified constraints. The process involves:

while there are untried tours
{
generate the next tour
if this tour covers all squares
{
print this path;
}
}

Backtracking Algorithm:

Backtracking operates incrementally, starting with an empty solution vector. Items are added one at a time, with each item representing a Knight's move. Upon addition, a check is performed to ensure it adheres to the constraints. If a violation occurs, the item is removed, and an alternative is attempted. If no alternatives work, backtracking occurs to the previous stage, removing the added item. If backtracking reaches the initial stage, indicating no solution, the process concludes. If the constraints are upheld, more items are added recursively, one at a time. Upon obtaining a complete solution vector, the solution is printed.

Here is the Backtracking algorithm for the Knight's Tour

problem:
  If all the squares are visited
  print the solution
  Else
  a) Add another to the solution vector and recursively
  check if it leads to a solution. (A Knight can make no more than
  eight moves. One of those eight moves is chosen in this step).
  b) If the move chosen doesn't lead to a solution
  then remove it from the solution vector and try another move.
  c) If none of the moves work, return false (Returning false
  removes the previously added item in recursion, and if false is
  returned by the initial call of recursion, "no solution exists")

The provided code demonstrates the implementation of the Knight's Tour problem using C++. The output is a 2D matrix (8*8) displaying numbers from 0 to 63, indicating the Knight's moves.

In terms of time complexity, considering N^2 squares with eight possible moves each, the worst-case running time is $O(N^2)$. The space complexity involves an auxiliary space of $O(N^2)$.

Subset Sum Challenge

The challenge posed by the subset sum problem involves identifying a subset of elements from a given set, where the sum of the selected elements equals a specified value, K. For our purposes, the set's values are non-negative, and the input set is assumed to be unique with no duplicates.

Exhaustive Approach: One method to find subsets summing up to K is to examine every conceivable subset. The powerset, with a size of 2^N, encompasses all generated subsets from a specified subset.

Backtracking Strategy: While exhaustive search considers all subsets, regardless of constraint satisfaction, backtracking allows for the systematic consideration of elements to be selected. Imagine a set with four elements, denoted as w[1] … w[4]. A backtracking algorithm, visualized through a tree diagram, generates a variable-sized tuple:

In this tree representation, each node signifies a function call, and branches represent candidate elements. The root node's four children correspond to each element in the set.

As we traverse down the tree, each level's branches represent tuple elements. For instance, at level 1, tuple_vector[1] can adopt values from the four branches. At level 2, tuple_vector[2] considers values from three branches, and so forth.

The left-most child of the root generates subsets with w[1], and the second child produces subsets with w[2] but without w[1]. Elements are added as we descend the tree, and if the added sum adheres to constraints, child nodes are generated. If constraints aren't met, no further subtrees are produced, and backtracking to unexplored nodes occurs.

Here's a pseudocode representation:
if (subset satisfies constraint)
print the subset
exclude the current element and consider the next element
else
generate nodes of the current level along the breadth of the tree and

recur for the next levels

Next, an implementation of subset sum using a variable-sized tuple vector is examined. This program explores possibilities akin to exhaustive search but optimizes through backtracking. The code demonstrates how backtracking solutions can be enhanced.

Backtracking shines when combining implicit and explicit constraints, halting node generation upon check failures. The algorithm gains efficiency by strengthening constraint checks and utilizing presorted data. In a presorted array, once the sum significantly exceeds the target number, the remaining array can be ignored, allowing backtracking to explore alternative possibilities.

Assuming a presorted array, the optimized implementation prunes the subtree if constraints are unmet:

```
#include
using namespace std;
#define ARRAYSIZE(a) (sizeof(a))/(sizeof(a[0]))

// ... (code for other functions, including printSubset, comparator, etc.)

int main()
{
int weights[] = {15, 22, 14, 26, 32, 9, 16, 8};
int target = 53;
int size = ARRAYSIZE(weights);
generateSubsets(weights, size, target);
```

cout « "Nodes generated " « total_nodes;
return 0;
}

Output:
8 9 14 22
8 14 15 16
15 16 22
Nodes generated 68

Considerations for fixed-size tuple analogs and binary pattern tree generation, with pruning for constraint non-satisfaction, open avenues for further exploration in solving the subset sum problem.

9

Conclusion

I appreciate your time in exploring my guide. In today's world, algorithms play a central role, addressing various everyday challenges. Often, these processes operate discreetly in the background, seamlessly delivering the desired outcomes as if by magic.

We initiated this journey with a swift examination of algorithm design, a crucial prerequisite before embarking on your own endeavors. Subsequently, we delved into prominent design techniques such as backtracking, recursion, branch and bound, and the divide and conquer algorithm. Abundant code examples were provided, offering a practical understanding of their functionality.

Moving forward, you can deepen your comprehension by immersing yourself further in these algorithms, bringing you a step closer to your objectives. Whether you aspire to grasp the intricacies behind the scenes or pursue a career in computer science, this book has furnished you with foundational knowledge.

Once again, thank you for your readership. I trust you found the book valuable.

www.ingramcontent.com/pod-product-compliance
Lightning Source LLC
LaVergne TN
LVHW020422080526
838202LV00055B/4997